INSPIRAT

Grandmothers

© 2008 by Barbour Publishing, Inc.

Compiled by Conover Swofford.

ISBN 978-1-60260-198-7

Some material previously published in *365 Favorite Quotes for Grandmothers* and *365 Inspirational Quotes*, published by Barbour Publishing, Inc.

All scripture quotations, unless otherwise noted, are taken from the King James Version of the Bible.

Scripture quotations marked NIV are taken from the HOLY BIBLE, NEW INTERNATIONAL VERSION®. NIV®. Copyright © 1973, 1978, 1984 by International Bible Society. Used by permission of Zondervan. All rights reserved.

Published by Barbour Publishing, Inc., P.O. Box 719, Uhrichsville, Ohio 44683, www.barbourbooks.com

Our mission is to publish and distribute inspirational products offering exceptional value and biblical encouragement to the masses.

 Member of the
Evangelical Christian
Publishers Association

Printed in China.

INSPIRATION FOR
Grandmothers

BARBOUR

Grandmas hold our tiny hands for just a little while. . .but our hearts forever.

UNKNOWN

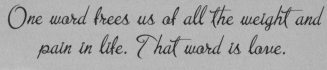

One word frees us of all the weight and pain in life. That word is love.

SOPHOCLES

*She openeth her mouth with wisdom;
and in her tongue is the law of kindness.*

PROVERBS 31:26

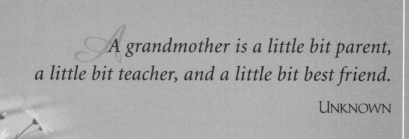

A grandmother is a little bit parent, a little bit teacher, and a little bit best friend.

UNKNOWN

If you want children to keep their feet on the ground,
put some responsibility on their shoulders.

ABIGAIL VAN BUREN

Therefore choose life, that both thou and thy seed may live: that thou mayest love the Lord thy God, and that thou mayest obey his voice, and that thou mayest cleave unto him: for he is thy life, and the length of thy days.

DEUTERONOMY 30:19-20

God cannot give us a happiness and peace apart from Himself because it is not there. There is no such thing.

C. S. LEWIS

Just about the time a woman thinks her work is done, she becomes a grandmother.

EDWARD H. DRESCHNACK

*Start by doing what's necessary,
then what's possible, and suddenly you
are doing the impossible.*

FRANCIS OF ASSISI

The LORD thy God in the midst of thee is mighty; he will save, he will rejoice over thee with joy; he will rest in his love, he will joy over thee with singing.

ZEPHANIAH 3:17

We turn not older with years
but newer every day.

EMILY DICKINSON

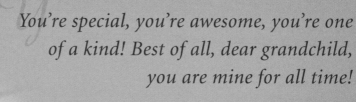

You're special, you're awesome, you're one of a kind! Best of all, dear grandchild, you are mine for all time!

KAREN HILL

Before me, even as behind,
God is, and all is well.

JOHN GREENLEAF WHITTIER

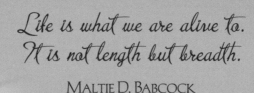

Life is what we are alive to.
It is not length but breadth.

MALTIE D. BABCOCK

Every good gift and every perfect gift is from above, and cometh down from the Father of lights, with whom is no variableness, neither shadow of turning.

JAMES 1:17

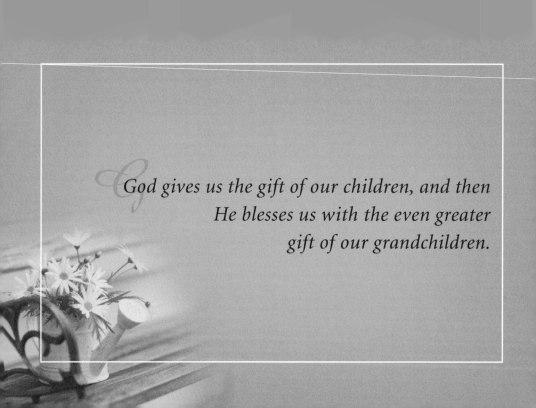

God gives us the gift of our children, and then He blesses us with the even greater gift of our grandchildren.

*When I approach a child, he inspires
in me two sentiments: tenderness for what he is,
and respect for what he may become.*

LOUIS PASTEUR

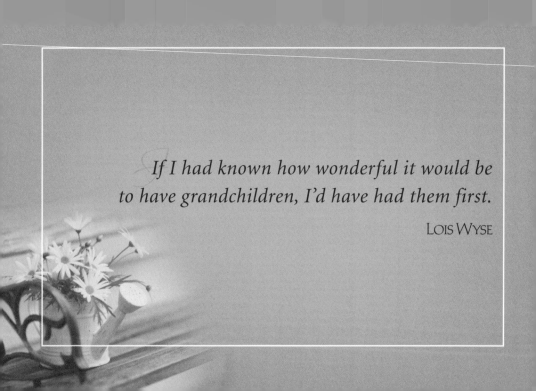

If I had known how wonderful it would be to have grandchildren, I'd have had them first.

LOIS WYSE

One of the most difficult things to give away
is kindness; it usually comes back to you.

ANONYMOUS

*When we do the best that we can,
we never know what miracle is wrought in our life,
or in the life of another.*

HELEN KELLER

You don't choose your family. They are God's gift to you, as you are to them.

DESMOND TUTU

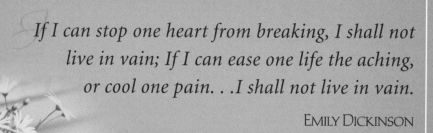

If I can stop one heart from breaking, I shall not live in vain; If I can ease one life the aching, or cool one pain. . .I shall not live in vain.

EMILY DICKINSON

*Therefore, as God's chosen people,
holy and dearly loved, clothe yourselves with
compassion, kindness, humility, gentleness and
patience. . . . Forgive as the Lord forgave you.*

COLOSSIANS 3:12-13 NIV

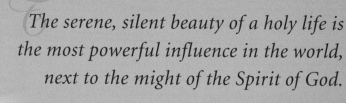

The serene, silent beauty of a holy life is the most powerful influence in the world, next to the might of the Spirit of God.

BLAISE PASCAL

The secret of happiness is to make others believe they are the cause of it.

UNKNOWN

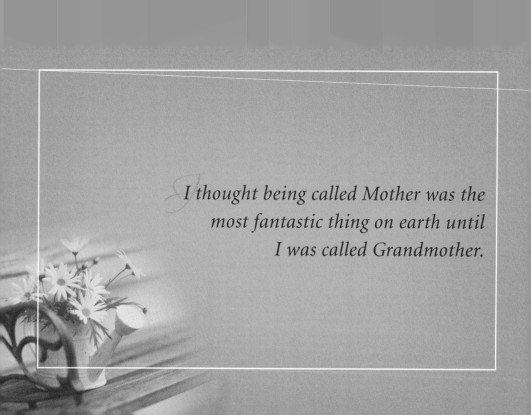

I thought being called Mother was the most fantastic thing on earth until I was called Grandmother.

What do we live for if it is not to make
life less difficult for each other?

GEORGE ELIOT

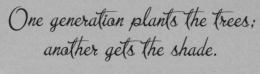

One generation plants the trees;
another gets the shade.

CHINESE PROVERB

Nothing you do for children is ever wasted.
They seem not to notice us, hovering,
averting our eyes, and they seldom offer thanks,
but what we do for them is never wasted.

GARRISON KEILLOR

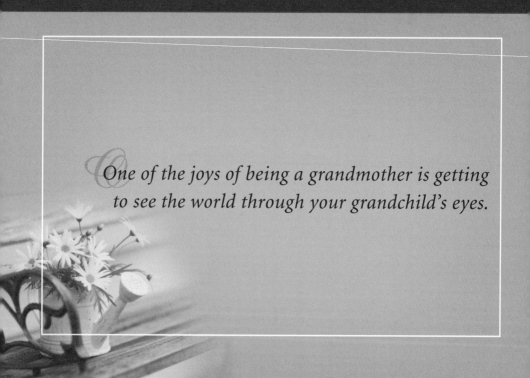

One of the joys of being a grandmother is getting to see the world through your grandchild's eyes.

*The important things are children,
honesty, integrity, and faith.*

ANDY WILLIAMS

Her children arise up, and call her blessed.

PROVERBS 31:28

We need to love our family for who they are and not for what they do.

KAREN MCDUFFY

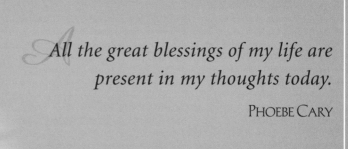

All the great blessings of my life are present in my thoughts today.

PHOEBE CARY

Our grandchildren are the
treasures of our hearts.

One of the greatest joys of being a grandmother
is holding your sleeping grandchild.

A child's hand in yours—what tenderness it arouses, what power it conjures. You are instantly the very touchstone of wisdom and strength.

MARJORIE HOLMES

It is as grandmothers that our mothers come into the fullness of their grace.

CHRISTOPHER MORLEY

Nobody can do for little children what grandparents do. Grandparents sort of sprinkle stardust over the lives of little children.

ALEX HALEY

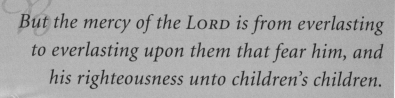

But the mercy of the LORD is from everlasting to everlasting upon them that fear him, and his righteousness unto children's children.

PSALM 103:17

Being a mother is the most important job in the world, but being a grandmother is the most fun.

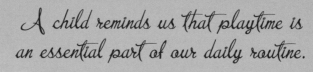

*A child reminds us that playtime is
an essential part of our daily routine.*

ANONYMOUS

Grandma always made you feel she had been waiting to see just you all day and now the day was complete.

MARCY DEMAREE

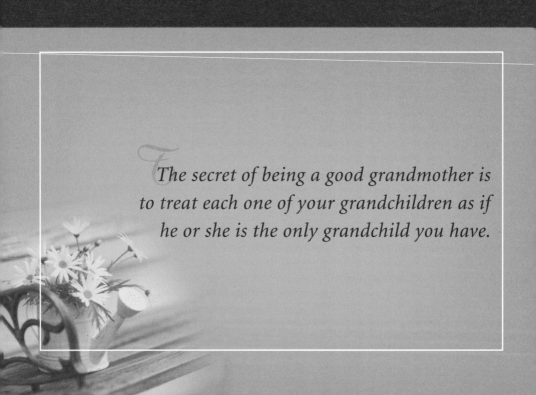

The secret of being a good grandmother is to treat each one of your grandchildren as if he or she is the only grandchild you have.

It's such a grand thing to be a mother of a mother—
that's why the world calls her grandmother.

UNKNOWN

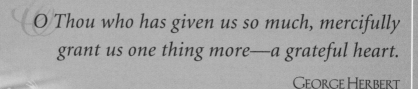

O Thou who has given us so much, mercifully grant us one thing more—a grateful heart.

George Herbert

There's no place like home
except Grandma's.

UNKNOWN

Do all the good you can, by all the means you can, in all the ways you can, in all the places you can, at all the times you can, to all the people you can, as long as ever you can.

JOHN WESLEY

Being confident of this very thing,
that he which hath begun a good work in you
will perform it until the day of Jesus Christ.

PHILIPPIANS 1:6

I try to avoid looking forward or backward, and try to keep looking upward.

CHARLOTTE BRONTË

True happiness. . .is not attained through self-gratification, but through fidelity to a worthy purpose.

HELEN KELLER

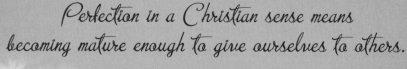

Perfection in a Christian sense means
becoming mature enough to give ourselves to others.

KATHLEEN NORRIS

This one thing I do, forgetting those things which are behind, and reaching forth unto those things which are before, I press toward the mark for the prize of the high calling of God in Christ Jesus.

PHILIPPIANS 3:13-14

It is not how many years we live,
but what we do with them.

CATHERINE BOOTH

*I have learned from experience that
the greater part of our happiness or misery
depends on our dispositions and
not on our circumstances.*

MARTHA WASHINGTON

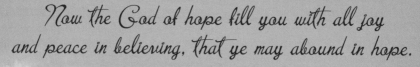

Now the God of hope fill you with all joy
and peace in believing, that ye may abound in hope.

ROMANS 15:13

We walk without fear, full of hope and courage and strength to do His will, waiting for the endless good which He is always giving as fast as He can get us able to take it in.

GEORGE MACDONALD

Always be in a state of expectancy, and see that you leave room for God to come in as He likes.

OSWALD CHAMBERS

The birth of a grandchild is a wonderful and exciting event! That wonder and excitement continues throughout life.

TOM POTTS

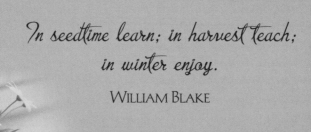

In seedtime learn; in harvest teach;
in winter enjoy.

WILLIAM BLAKE

We won't always know whose lives we touched and made better for our having cared, because actions can sometimes have unforeseen ramifications. What's important is that you do care and you act.

CHARLOTTE LUNSFORD

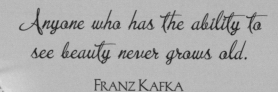

*Anyone who has the ability to
see beauty never grows old.*

FRANZ KAFKA

Love cannot remain by itself—
it has no meaning. Love has to be put into
action, and that action is service.

MOTHER TERESA

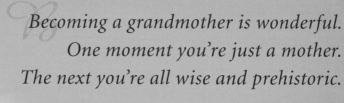

Becoming a grandmother is wonderful.
One moment you're just a mother.
The next you're all wise and prehistoric.

PAM BROWN

*Grandmother—a wonderful mother
with lots of practice.*

UNKNOWN

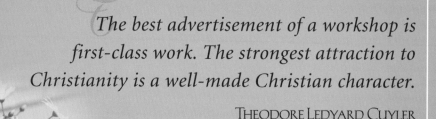

The best advertisement of a workshop is first-class work. The strongest attraction to Christianity is a well-made Christian character.

THEODORE LEDYARD CUYLER

Family faces are magic mirrors.
Looking at people who belong to us,
we see the past, present, and future.

GAIL LUMET BUCKLEY

Your family and your love must be cultivated like a garden. Time, effort, and imagination must be summoned constantly to keep any relationship flourishing and growing.

JIM ROBIN

I thank my God upon every remembrance of you.

PHILIPPIANS 1:3

The greatest possession we have costs nothing;
it's known as love.

BRIAN JETT

Wherefore seeing we also are compassed about with so great a cloud of witnesses, let us lay aside every weight, and the sin which doth so easily beset us, and let us run with patience the race that is set before us, looking unto Jesus the author and finisher of our faith.

HEBREWS 12:1-2

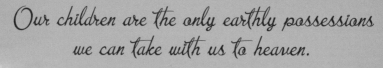

Our children are the only earthly possessions
we can take with us to heaven.

OUR DAILY BREAD

Faith in small things has repercussions that ripple all the way out. In a huge, dark room a little match can light up the place.

JONI EARECKSON TADA

We learn from raising our own children
how to be perfect grandmothers.

When we accept tough jobs as a challenge and wade into them with joy and enthusiasm, miracles can happen.

ARLAND GILBERT

Life's blows cannot break a person whose spirit
is warmed at the fire of enthusiasm.

NORMAN VINCENT PEALE

Holding a great-grandchild makes getting old worthwhile.

EVALYN RIKKERS

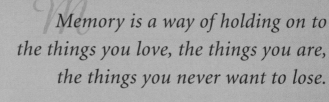

Memory is a way of holding on to the things you love, the things you are, the things you never want to lose.

KEVIN ARNOLD, *THE WONDER YEARS*

What a joy to share our memories with
the newest generation in our families.

A young child is, indeed, a true scientist, just one big question mark. What? Why? How? I never cease to marvel at the recurring miracle of growth, to be fascinated by the mystery and wonder of this brave enthusiasm.

VICTORIA WAGNER

Christianity is not a theory or speculation,
but a life; not a philosophy of life,
but a life and a living process.

SAMUEL TAYLOR COLERIDGE

Faith makes all things possible. . . .
Love makes all things easy.

DWIGHT L. MOODY

The aged women likewise, that they be in behaviour as becometh holiness, not false accusers, not given to much wine, teachers of good things; that they may teach the young women to be sober, to love their husbands, to love their children, to be discreet, chaste, keepers at home, good, obedient to their own husbands, that the word of God be not blasphemed.

TITUS 2:3-5

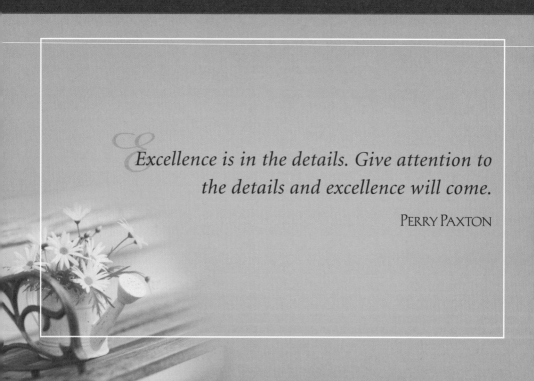

Excellence is in the details. Give attention to the details and excellence will come.

PERRY PAXTON

We can learn as much from our grandchildren
as they can learn from us.

"And a little child shall lead them."

ISAIAH 11:6

Our grandchildren accept us for ourselves, without rebuke or effort to change us, as no one in our entire lives has ever done, not our parents, siblings, spouses, friends—and hardly ever our own grown children.

RUTH GOODE

Train up a child in the way he should go:
and when he is old, he will not depart from it.

PROVERBS 22:6

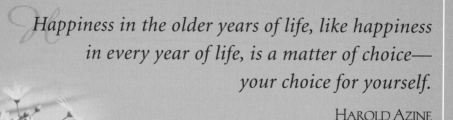

Happiness in the older years of life, like happiness in every year of life, is a matter of choice—your choice for yourself.

HAROLD AZINE

*The cheerful live longest in years,
and afterward in our regards.
Cheerfulness is the offshoot of goodness.*

CHRISTIAN NESTELL BOVEE

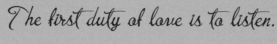

The first duty of love is to listen.

PAUL TILLICH

*Your best harvest may be the pleasure
you get from working with family and friends.
There's never a shortage of things to do,
no limit to the lessons that can be learned.*

STEVEN WILLSON

*If we listen to our children and our grandchildren,
we will discover amazing things.*

We are not the same persons this year as last; nor are those we love. It is a happy chance if we, changing, continue to love as a changed person.

W. SOMERSET MAUGHAM

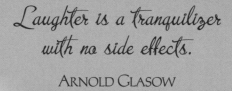

*Laughter is a tranquilizer
with no side effects.*

ARNOLD GLASOW

Trust in the LORD with all thine heart;
and lean not unto thine own understanding.
In all thy ways acknowledge him,
and he shall direct thy paths.

PROVERBS 3:5-6

O Thou who dwellest in so many homes, possess Thyself of this. Bless the life that is sheltered here. Grant that trust and peace and comfort abide within, and that love and life and usefulness may go out from this home forever.

UNKNOWN

Lo, children are an heritage of the Lord.

PSALM 127:3

When a child is born, so are grandmothers.

JUDITH LEVY

I refer to my grandchildren as my "hilarious heritage." As one of them once told me, they keep me "giggled up." I love being around them because they are so funny.

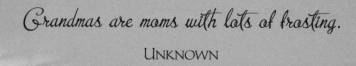

Grandmas are moms with lots of frosting.

UNKNOWN

I am not what I ought to be. I am not what I wish to be. I am not even what I hope to be. But by the cross of Christ, I am not what I was.

JOHN NEWTON

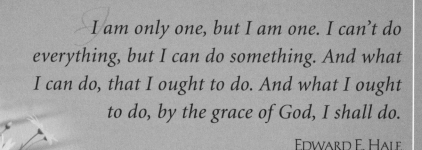

I am only one, but I am one. I can't do everything, but I can do something. And what I can do, that I ought to do. And what I ought to do, by the grace of God, I shall do.

EDWARD E. HALE

Take my life, and let it be consecrated,
Lord, to Thee.

FRANCES R. HAVERGAL

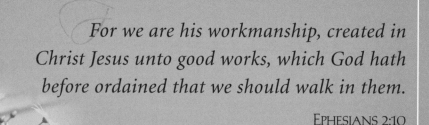

For we are his workmanship, created in Christ Jesus unto good works, which God hath before ordained that we should walk in them.

EPHESIANS 2:10

The true call of a Christian is not
to do extraordinary things but to do ordinary
things in an extraordinary way.

DEAN STANLEY

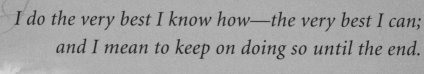

*I do the very best I know how—the very best I can;
and I mean to keep on doing so until the end.*

ABRAHAM LINCOLN

Grandmas never run out of hugs or cookies.

UNKNOWN

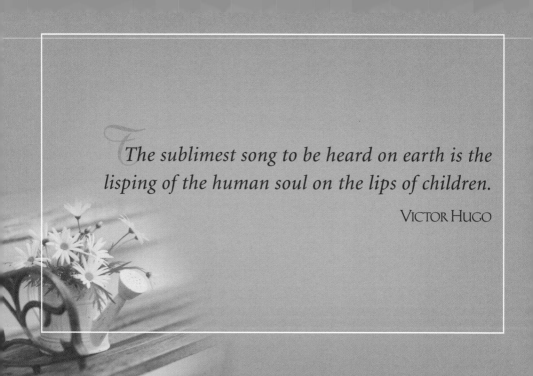

The sublimest song to be heard on earth is the lisping of the human soul on the lips of children.

VICTOR HUGO

*A grandma's name is little less in love
than is the doting title of a mother.*

WILLIAM SHAKESPEARE

*The world will not care what we know
until they know we care.*

GENE BARRON

Love is optimistic; it looks at people in the best light. Love thinks constructively as it senses the grand possibilities in other people.

GEORGE SWEETING

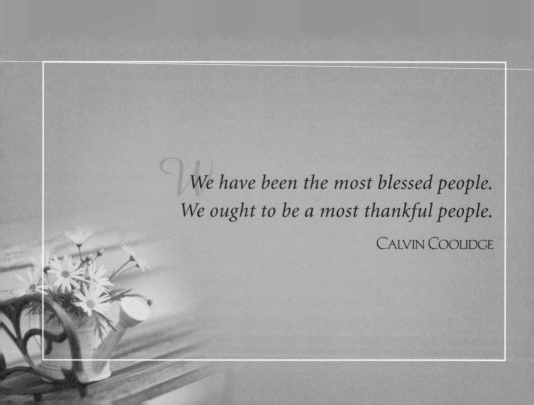

We have been the most blessed people.
We ought to be a most thankful people.

CALVIN COOLIDGE

Is there any greater joy in life than
watching our children's children becoming what
God intended them to be?

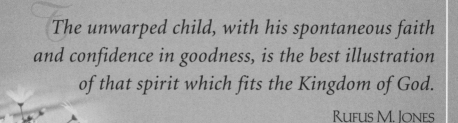

The unwarped child, with his spontaneous faith and confidence in goodness, is the best illustration of that spirit which fits the Kingdom of God.

RUFUS M. JONES

Children—the fruit of the seeds
of all your finest hopes.

GLORIA GAITHER

God's love for poor sinners is wonderful, but God's patience with ill-natured saints is a deeper mystery.

HENRY DRUMMOND

Sometimes we need the patience of God to deal with our grandchildren.

*This is one of the miracles of love: It gives. . .
a power of seeing through its own enchantments
and yet not being disenchanted.*

C. S. LEWIS

The first great gift we can bestow
on others is a good example.

THOMAS MORELL

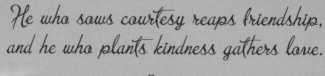

He who sows courtesy reaps friendship,
and he who plants kindness gathers love.

BASIL

For even hereunto were ye called: because Christ also suffered for us, leaving us an example, that ye should follow his steps.

1 PETER 2:21

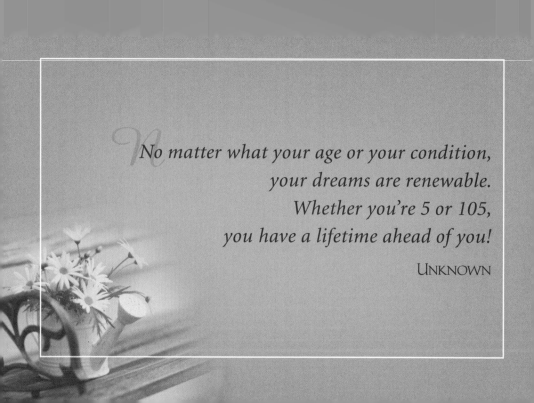

*No matter what your age or your condition,
your dreams are renewable.
Whether you're 5 or 105,
you have a lifetime ahead of you!*

Unknown

He does most in God's great world who does his best in his own little world.

THOMAS JEFFERSON

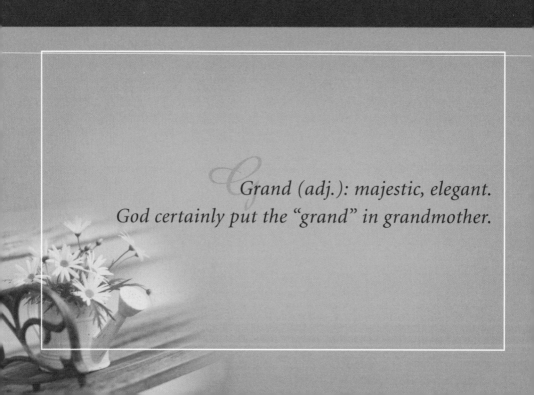

Grand (adj.): majestic, elegant.
God certainly put the "grand" in grandmother.

*Every child is a miracle unfolding,
and the joy of being a grandmother is
watching and helping that miracle.*

All God's glory and beauty come from within, and there He delights to dwell. His visits there are frequent, His conversation sweet, His comforts refreshing, His peace passing all understanding.

THOMAS Á KEMPIS

Let my soul take refuge. . .beneath the shadow of Your wings; let my heart, this sea of restless waves, find peace in You, O God.

<small>AUGUSTINE</small>

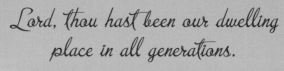

Lord, thou hast been our dwelling
place in all generations.

Psalm 90:1

We were not sent into this world to do anything into which we cannot put our hearts.

JOHN RUSKIN

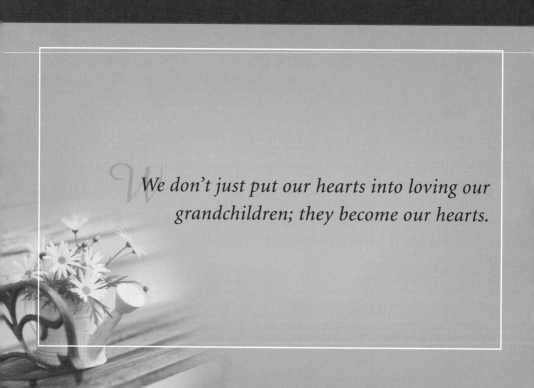

We don't just put our hearts into loving our grandchildren; they become our hearts.

Time, indeed, is a sacred gift,
and each day is a little life.

JOHN LUBBOCK

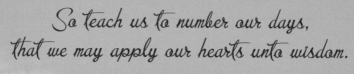

So teach us to number our days,
that we may apply our hearts unto wisdom.

PSALM 90:12

Teaching our grandchildren to make the most of their time is perhaps one of the best things we can teach them.

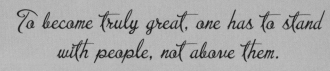

To become truly great, one has to stand
with people, not above them.

CHARLES DE MONTESQUIEU

The LORD bless thee, and keep thee:
the LORD make his face shine upon thee,
and be gracious unto thee: the LORD lift up his
countenance upon thee, and give thee peace.

NUMBERS 6:24-26

The Lord blessed us with grandchildren.
It is our joy to be a blessing to them.

It is not in the still calm of life,
or in the repose of a specific situation,
that great characters are formed.

ABIGAIL ADAMS

As much as we are trying to help our grandchildren form their characters, God is using them to help us form our own characters.

I want to help you to grow as beautiful as
God meant you to be when He thought of you first.

GEORGE MACDONALD

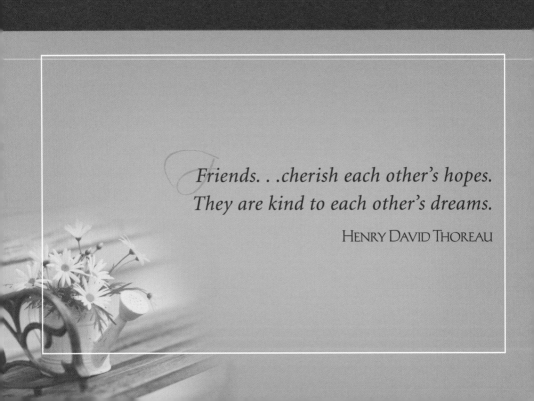

Friends. . .cherish each other's hopes.
They are kind to each other's dreams.

HENRY DAVID THOREAU

The beauty seen is partly in him who sees it.

CHRISTIAN NESTELL BOVEE

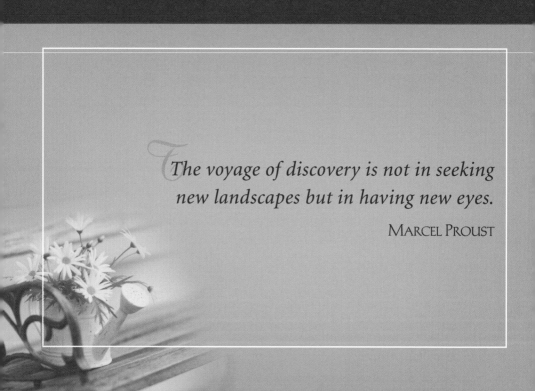

The voyage of discovery is not in seeking new landscapes but in having new eyes.

MARCEL PROUST

How delightful to see life through
the eyes of our grandchildren.

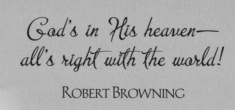

God's in His heaven—
all's right with the world!

ROBERT BROWNING

There is no duty we so much underrate as the duty of being happy. By being happy we sow anonymous benefits upon the world.

ROBERT LOUIS STEVENSON

*Let there be many windows in your soul,
that all the glory of the universe may beautify it.*

ELLA WHEELER WILCOX

Begin at once to live, and count each day as a separate life.

SENECA

*And if tonight my soul may find her peace in sleep,
and sink in good oblivion, and in the morning wake
like a new-opened flower, then I have been
dipped again in God, and new-created.*

D. H. LAWRENCE

Thou wilt shew me the path of life:
in thy presence is fulness of joy; at thy right hand
there are pleasures for evermore.

PSALM 16:11

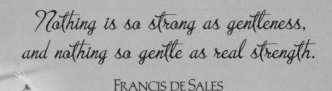

Nothing is so strong as gentleness,
and nothing so gentle as real strength.

FRANCIS DE SALES

*Though we travel the world over
to find the beautiful, we must carry it
with us or we find it not.*

RALPH WALDO EMERSON

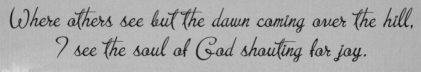

Where others see but the dawn coming over the hill,
I see the soul of God shouting for joy.

WILLIAM BLAKE

*This is the day which the L*ORD *hath made; we will rejoice and be glad in it.*

PSALM 118:24

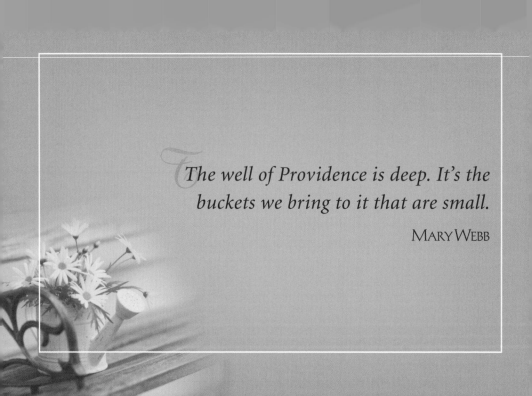

The well of Providence is deep. It's the buckets we bring to it that are small.

MARY WEBB

*Our chief end is to glorify God
and to enjoy Him forever.*

PRESBYTERIAN CATECHISM

We have a God who delights in impossibilities.

ANDREW MURRAY

*It isn't the goal that shapes us;
it is the journey we take on our way to the goal
that makes us what we are.*

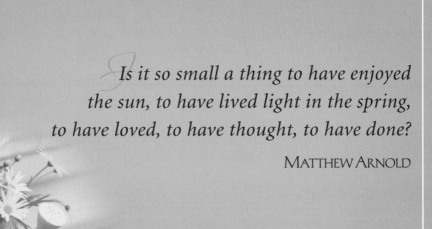

Is it so small a thing to have enjoyed the sun, to have lived light in the spring, to have loved, to have thought, to have done?

MATTHEW ARNOLD

There is a past which is gone forever,
but there is a future which is still our own.

F. W. ROBERTSON

The joy of the Lord is your strength.

NEHEMIAH 8:10

*To be a joy-bearer and a joy-giver
says everything, for in our life, if one is joyful,
it means that one is faithfully living for God,
and that nothing else counts; and if one gives
joy to others, one is doing God's work.*

JANET ERSKINE STUART

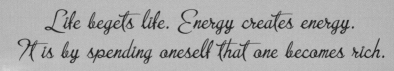

Life begets life. Energy creates energy.
It is by spending oneself that one becomes rich.

SARAH BERNHARDT

May your life become one of glad and unending praise to the Lord as you journey through this world, and in the world that is to come!

TERESA OF AVILA

God's designs regarding you, and His methods of bringing about those designs, are infinitely wise.

JEANNE GUYON

Give thanks for unknown blessings
already on their way.

NATIVE AMERICAN PROVERB

Whether sixty or sixteen, there is in every human being's heart the love of wonder; the sweet amazement at the stars and starlike things, the undaunted challenge of events, the unfailing childlike appetite for what-next, and the joy of the game of living.

SAMUEL ULLMAN

Seek the LORD and his strength,
seek his face continually. Remember his
marvellous works that he hath done, his wonders,
and the judgments of his mouth.

1 CHRONICLES 16:11-12

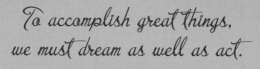

To accomplish great things,
we must dream as well as act.

ANATOLE FRANCE

The best things are nearest:
breath in your nostrils, light in your eyes,
flowers at your feet, duties at your hand,
the path of God just before you.

ROBERT LOUIS STEVENSON

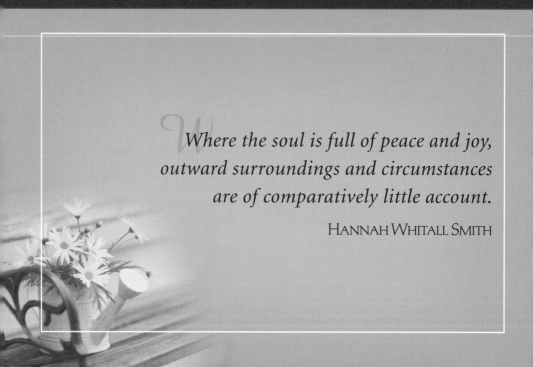

*Where the soul is full of peace and joy,
outward surroundings and circumstances
are of comparatively little account.*

Hannah Whitall Smith

Our Lord does not care so much for
the importance of our works as for the love
with which they are done.

TERESA OF AVILA

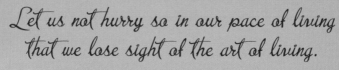

Let us not hurry so in our pace of living
that we lose sight of the art of living.

FRANCIS BACON

Everyone has a unique role to fill in the world and is important in some respect. Everyone, including and perhaps especially you, is indispensable.

NATHANIEL HAWTHORNE

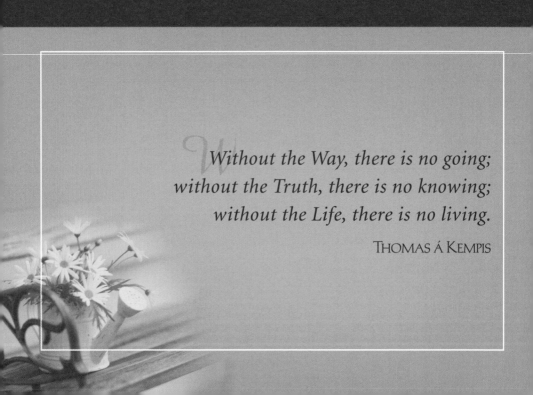

*Without the Way, there is no going;
without the Truth, there is no knowing;
without the Life, there is no living.*

THOMAS Á KEMPIS

A gentle word, a kind look, a good-natured smile can work wonders and accomplish miracles.

WILLIAM HAZLITT

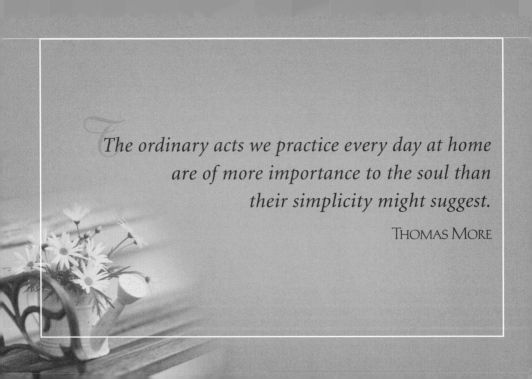

The ordinary acts we practice every day at home are of more importance to the soul than their simplicity might suggest.

THOMAS MORE

The smallest bit of obedience
opens heaven, and the deepest truths of
God immediately become ours.

OSWALD CHAMBERS

The riches that are in the heart cannot be stolen.

RUSSIAN PROVERB

*In a world where there is so much to be done,
I felt strongly impressed that there must
be something for me to do.*

DOROTHEA DIX

After the verb "to love," "to help" is the most beautiful verb in the world.

BERTHA VON SUTTNER

Think. . .of the world you carry within you.

RAINER MARIA RILKE

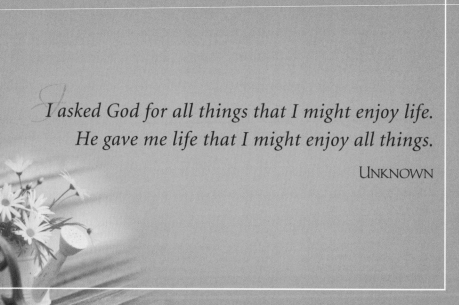

I asked God for all things that I might enjoy life.
He gave me life that I might enjoy all things.

UNKNOWN

Eye hath not seen, nor ear heard, neither have entered into the heart of man, the things which God hath prepared for them that love him.

1 CORINTHIANS 2:9

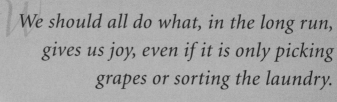

We should all do what, in the long run, gives us joy, even if it is only picking grapes or sorting the laundry.

E. B. WHITE

I don't believe makeup and the right hairstyle alone can make a woman beautiful. The most radiant woman in the room is the one full of life and experience.

UNKNOWN

Beauty is whatever gives joy.

EDNA ST. VINCENT MILLAY

Let the beauty of the LORD *our God be upon us:
and establish thou the work of our hands upon us;
yea, the work of our hands establish thou it.*

PSALM 90:17